Bill Reynolds

CORVETTE
America's Most Exciting Sportscar

Bill Reynolds

CORVETTE
America's Most Exciting Sportscar

CRESCENT BOOKS
NEW YORK • AVENEL, NEW JERSEY

Featuring the photography of Nicky Wright

CLB 2982
© 1993 Colour Library Books Ltd., Godalming, Surrey, England
This 1993 edition published by Crescent Books
distributed by Outlet Book Company, Inc.,
a Random House Company,
40 Engelhard Avenue, Avenel, New Jersey 07001
Printed and bound in Hong Kong
ISBN 0 517 07293 9
8 7 6 5 4 3 2 1

America's Sports Car

The Corvette is a proper, brutal sports car that eats and breathes fire, and has enough power to get inexperienced or careless drivers into trouble. To the true *aficionado*, the fact that most Corvettes have also looked good is secondary. The important thing is that a true sports car should be quick, both off the mark and in the bends, and that it should reward proper skill with proper response. If you overcook it on the corners, and the car turns around and bites you, that merely increases your respect for it.

The English, traditionally the foremost makers of such vehicles, have a wonderful description for real sports cars. They call them "hairy men's cars." The kind of car that you can steer with the wheel or with the accelerator – or even with the handbrake, if you're really good – leads to what is commonly called a "hairy" style of driving. "Hairy" is not a term bestowed lightly. Corvettes are undeniably hairy!

There is no doubt that in one area or another some Corvettes have been very much better than others. For years, they were terrifyingly underbraked. For example, with hard driving on a twisty road, diligently applying the boot to the loud pedal and the brake in turn would cause the drums to overheat and to fade to nigh impotence. The '58s, for all the nostalgia they command today, were quite properly seen at the time of their release as grossly over-chromed and over-styled. The understandable fear was that the performance aspect would be forgotten, and the car would become just another Detroit showboat – a cross between a display of cheap cutlery and a rubber dinghy on roller skates! The Sting Ray badly needed a front air dam to keep the nose on the ground, and all of the "Mako Shark" series were prone to overheating, and so forth.

But to a large extent, this is actually a part of the attraction of the Corvette. The compromises have been mercifully few – the fake air scoops and the other features that the "stylists" have tried to foist upon the hapless sports-car enthusiast have, for the most part, been eclipsed by the power, the traction, and the sheer *hairiness* of the whole thing. If people didn't like the harshness of the suspension, well, tough – rock-hard suspension was traditionally the price you paid for precise handling, and if you wanted a "wallowmobile," you could go buy something else.

Of course there were creative and commercial conflicts between the men who knew how to build sports cars (for the Corvette, the memorable figure was Zora Arkus-Duntov) and the men who knew how to sell domestic appliances, which is about what the everyday automobile amounts to. Mercifully, though, there were noble exceptions to the domestic-appliance brigade, too, and for the Corvette, the name of Ed Cole springs immediately to mind. Then there were the hard-core stylists like Bill Mitchell, whose background was in art rather than in engineering and who was Vice President for Design. He was the one who was responsible for the clearly lethal, split rear window on the original Sting Ray. Despite various corporate road-bumps, though, there were enough people at Chevrolet who kept the faith, and who saw to it that the Corvette remained a sports car, or at the very least, an extremely quick Grand Tourer.

The most important general point to make at this stage is that we cannot judge the past by the standards of the present. Today, in an age when 186 mph (300 kph) is rapidly becoming the standard for anything with pretensions to being a "Supercar," and where 200 mph (323 kph) is the target, top speeds like 120-130 mph seem absurdly slow. But 20 years ago, 130 mph was fast and 140 mph was very fast.

A second point, almost as important, is that we should not be blinded by everything that is put out by the many motoring journalists. Quite apart from straightforward technical errors, too many writers try to make themselves look important by claiming skills they do not have. Ninety-nine per cent of the remarks about "persistent oversteer at 140 mph" are untrue. At very high speeds, serious handling flaws would simply kill the vast majority of the motoring press and they would not have a snowball's chance in hell of correcting whatever problems arose.

For my own credentials, I drive (and ride fast motorcycles) on both sides of the Atlantic, and I am no stranger to speeds of around two miles a minute or 200 kph, but I know that it takes me a long time to become sufficiently used to any vehicle to extract the maximum performance from it. I also know that a few hours, or even a few minutes at a press-fest are not the time to do it. Besides, be honest, how often do you significantly exceed 100 mph (160 kph)? I need to keep my driver's license too badly to lose it on doing too much for too long! A motoring journalist's job – and my task in this book – is to convey some of the excitement, and some of the drawbacks, of driving cars that most people can only dream about.

In this book, I have borrowed Shakespeare's idea of the Seven Ages of Man, and applied them to the auto to give the Seven Ages of Corvette. So, in the beginning was the Motorama show car, which became the '53 Corvette. And the '53-'55 begat the '56-'57, which was the second generation. And the '56-'57 begat the '58-'62, which begat the '63-'67 Sting Ray, which begat the '68-'82 Mako Shark, and these were the third, fourth and fifth generations. In 1983 General Motors brought forth the Sixth Generation, which continued into the early 1990s. And at the time of writing, we were in daily expectation of the seventh generation, as we had been promised a mid-engined car. And whether the seventh generation should come in our time (for there had been signs from Bowling Green), or in the near future, we knew not!

Motorama and the First Corvettes

As early as 1952, Harley Earl – the legendary founder and head of General Motors' Art and Color Section – was predicting that Americans would soon forget about Limey imports such as MG and Jaguar once the new, sporty Chevys came out.

He may have been more than a little overconfident, but he was about to give the English a good run for their money. He was one of the first Americans to realize that the "dream car" creations of the great European *carrossiers* such as Saoutchik or Barker on chassis by names like Delage and Bentley could and should be countered by dream cars from the big American automobile companies. His '38 Buick "Y-Job" was prophetic, and gave rise to the "Motorama" traveling auto shows, but his Motorama two-seater sports car, first contemplated in early 1951, was to effectively sire a new brand of product.

Fortunately, instead of sticking too closely to production parts, and instead of treating it purely as a cosmetic exercise, Harley Earl turned the mechanical side of it over to Robert F. McLean, who had degrees in both engineering and industrial design from Cal Tech. McLean's prime goal was a 50/50 front/rear weight distribution for totally neutral handling, a difficult ideal to attain with any front-drive car, and a particularly difficult one in the days when American automobiles frequently had as much engine weight in front of the front axle as behind it. By setting the seats and motor as far back in the chassis as was decently possible, he achieved 53/47 per cent, which is still very tolerable today

and which was moreover achieved with a long, iron six-cylinder engine and conventional gearbox, instead of the rear transaxle which would be regarded as the obvious solution today.

The car was chassis-built, of course – the series-production, racing-car monocoque, was still years in the future – and for expediency, a hand-laid GRP shell was built. When in early 1952 a glass-fiber-bodied prototype was rolled in a big way, without significant damage, the decision was made to adopt GRP as the production body material – the decision made, literally "by accident!"

Although the X-frame chassis and the GRP body were new, the motor was not, it was no more than a hotted-up version of the pre-war 235.5 cid (3859 cc) straight-six pushrod motor. In standard trim, it produced 105 SAE bhp, maybe the equivalent of 90 DIN bhp, which was miserable even by the criteria of the time. The old SAE horsepower figures were at the crankshaft, without any engine ancillaries such as water pump or cooling fan and without the tiresome effects of any attempt to quiet the exhaust. GM's engineers did, however, manage to persuade the long-suffering motor to disburse 150 SAE bhp (probably well over 120 bhp DIN) by means of a number of expedients. These included a higher-lift, longer-duration cam borrowed from the truck line, solid push-rods instead of hydraulic valve operation, twin springs on each valve (allowing higher speeds without valve float), and of course those time-honored hot-rod tricks of a higher compression ratio (8:1 instead of 7.5:1). There was also a free-breathing dual exhaust and triple twin-choke Carter carbs.

At this point, according to Corvette lore, they ran into a problem which seems laughable today. They simply did not have a manual transmission that could handle all this searing power, so they used the two-speed Powerglide automatic. For comparison, the Jaguar XK engine (also a straight six, of 3442 cc, but with overhead cams) delivered 180 bhp in 1951 "special equipment" form, and fed that through a four-speed gearbox with electric overdrive! It may however be that this story is a myth, and it is quite possible that they saw automatics as the wave of the future and decided that their newest car should be offered with nothing else.

Another gruesome hangover from the past was recirculating-ball steering, albeit geared at what was for an American car of the period a quick 16:1. Rack-and-pinion was considered, but was dismissed as *too* quick at 10:1.

Classic vintage touches included the use of removable side-screens instead of wind-up windows, and built-in wire-mesh stone guards over the recessed headlights. A genuinely disagreeable feature was the imitation knock-on hub, which was just a wheel cover on a standard pressed-steel wheel.

Even with its faults, this was a car which attracted immense attention of the best possible kind when it first appeared at the January 1953 Motorama. Everyone asked the same questions: "When?" and "How Much?" To get those questions asked in *that order* GM really had to be doing something right.

The answer was one of indecision. Dealer net price was set at $2470 plus $248 delivery and handling, with a suggested retail of $3250. But in the same bulletin that set those prices, it was advised that "no dealer is in a position to accept firm deliveries for 1953." In other words, GM was going to practice making them for a while – the initial target was 50 a month – until they were confident enough to enter series production. The few that were made would (in theory) be sold to selected customers who might be expected to be leaders of opinion in their respective communities.

Two problems immediately became evident. One was that many people, including the press, wondered whether the Corvette was a real car or not – many, after all, still remembered the Tucker. They therefore kept a wary distance. The other problem was that "leaders of opinion" were not the people who were going to buy Corvettes. Mayors, well-established customers and other worthies were simply not the market to which the new car appealed. Several cars went to project engineers, the second wave went to GM managers and others inside the GM network, and not until 1954 did GM seriously begin to address the world at large. In the meanwhile, a load of rather predictable excitement from the GM publicity department had tried to keep interest alive, though actual road tests had vastly more influence.

It is difficult, almost four decades later, to "read" what these road tests said. *Road and Track* was enthusiastic and reasonably objective, though one cannot help feeling that their opinions were colored by an relief that the U.S.A. had started to make a serious, affordable, series-production sports car. At $3523 in 1954, the Corvette was roughly comparable in performance with the $4721 Nash-Healey – a second slower to 60 mph (97 kph), at 11 seconds instead of 10 seconds, but offering a 106 mph top speed instead of 105 mph (171 kph instead of 169 kph). The engine even grew another five bhp, for 155 bhp at 4200 rpm. But next to the significantly more expensive XK140, it was a slug. The basic XK engine was 190 bhp, and the SE (Special Equipment) version of the Jaguar could offer 210 bhp, 0-60 in under 8.5 seconds and a top speed in overdrive fourth of 130 mph (about 210 kph). Even the contemporary TR2, with only a two-liter engine, offered more top end than the Corvette and similar acceleration. The Corvette was good, but it was not great – people were not about to forget the Limey cars just yet. Sales were very low, and unsold '54 Corvettes hung around in dealers' lots all over America.

The Corvette would have died then and there if it had not been for a series of happy accidents. The appearance of Ford's Thunderbird in September 1954 was one. It introduced the "personal car" concept that would help to boost the two-car family. The second was the availability of the new 265 cid (4343 cc) V-8 that was due to appear in the 1955 model year. The third was the arrival of Zora Arkus-Duntov, a German who understood sports cars. Among his first acts were putting two degrees of positive caster on the front end, and moving the rear spring bushing, to improve the Corvette's handling drastically.

The result of fitting the new motor was a modest weight reduction from just over 2700 lb. to rather under 2700 lb., and a jump in power to 195 bhp. Torque also jumped from 223 lb.-ft. at 2400 rpm to 260 lb.-ft. at 3000 rpm. The 0-60 time accordingly fell from about 11 seconds to an XK 140-like eight and a half seconds, top speed rose to almost two miles a minute (190 kph), and fuel consumption was actually two to three mpg better than the old straight-six, and over 20 mpg (11 liters/100 km) was available to the reasonably restrained driver. Surprisingly, only about 43 per cent of '55 Corvettes were fitted with the V-8 – which also came with a 12-volt system instead of six-volt, and which could be supplied (towards the end of the year) with a three-speed manual box which was lighter than the old two-speed slushbox. Suddenly, for the '55 model year, the Corvette was a *serious* motor car, even if not many were sold.

Not a Thunderbird

Ford's original quick, light, elegant T-Bird was a serious challenge to the Corvette, the more so as the Ford sold some 16,000 units in 1955 compared with the Corvette's

700. But an almost Oriental question of "face" had been raised, and GM was determined not to "lose face."

Ford displayed their customary unerring disregard for automobiles, and their equally customary cynicism about the "bottom line," by downrating the sporty T-Bird to little more than a pretty compact, a route they would follow again, a decade later, with the Mustang. General Motors, by contrast, decided to show Ford what a *real* sports car went, and looked like, and by general consensus, they made the most handsome ever of all Corvettes.

The new Corvette appeared with what we now regard as the classic "coves" or rebates in the sides, wind-up windows (side-screens were considered a little too vintage), and more power. The standard V8 now delivered 210 bhp SAE at 5200 rpm, and if you went for the options, you could have 225 to 240 bhp obtained by means of hotter cams, a cast-alloy inlet tract, and twin four-barrel carbs in place of the old single unit. Weight had inevitably crept up to 2980 lb. (1355 kg), or 3080 lb. if you insisted on the Powerglide transmission, but as the 0-60 mph speed dropped to 7.3 seconds, the top speed rose to an easy 129 mph (208 kph).

As before, and as since, the Corvette was an odd blend of the elegant and the brutal. Bumping up the tire pressure by five psi front and back to 30 psi front, 32 psi rear, markedly improved the handling, but there was no 1950s "boulevard ride" even at the stock pressures. Because the steering was still recirculating-ball, there was an inch and a half (about 40 mm) of play in it, and stiffer, better-damped shocks on the rear end were all but mandatory for serious fast driving. But with all these faults, the Corvette was still a car you could "set up" for a corner. Once you had taken up the slack in the steering, and allowed the car to assume its natural roll angle, you could take it through a corner very quickly indeed. At Sebring in 1956, a stock Corvette complete with heater, radio and power roof was one of three finishers in the 12-hour Endurance. Of the other two Corvettes to finish, one won the Production Sports Car crown, and the other the prize for Modified Sports Car. In that particular race, 36 of the 60 entries fell by the wayside; so for Corvettes to account for one-eighth of the finishing field was no mean accomplishment. At Pebble Beach, in the same year, a modified Corvette came a close second, to nothing less than a legendary Mercedes-Benz 300 SL "Gullwing." If the Corvette had been equipped with brakes, it could even have won, but it was handicapped by its laughably narrow drums.

For 1957, GM took the route which seems so obvious with hindsight, but which seems so often to have eluded other manufacturers when faced with equally clear choices. They gave the beast more brakes – albeit only finned drums, instead of disks – and they gave it more reason to use them. The 265 cid engine was made available bored out to 283 cid (4583 cc), with 220 bhp in "cooking" form but with a range of options. These included fuel injection, which could take it out to 283 bhp, the sought-after 1 bhp per cubic inch, though it was still somewhat under 62 bhp/ liter. What was more, late in 1957 they finally offered what *aficionados* of imported European sports cars took for granted – a four-speed gearbox. The weight had crept up yet again, but you could still have all that power at under 2800 lb. (1273 kg), which translated into 222 bhp/tonne. This was a marked improvement of the 122 bhp/tonne of the original 1953 Corvette! The 0-60 mph time could now be dragged just below the six-second mark (though six to seven seconds would be the best that most drivers would be able to achieve), and the top speed could get into the mid-130s (almost 220 kph). Incidentally, power-to-weight figures are quoted here in bhp/tonne because the metric "tonne" of 2200 lb. (1000 kg) splits the difference between the 2000 lb. "short ton" and the 2240 lb. "long ton," and leaves no room for ambiguity.

Meanwhile, something very unpleasant happened, something which could quite easily have destroyed the Corvette completely, or turned it into a car that was all "show" and no "go." In June 1957, the Automobile Manufacturers' Association (AMA) adopted a resolution which required first, that all members cease and desist from any kind of advertising with a performance slant, and second, that they also withdraw all support from racing of any kind – not merely competition sponsorship, but technical assistance, too.

It was an illustration of corporate sanctimoniousness at its worst, and it is no exaggeration to say that the foundations of the problems which beset the American automobile industry today were laid at that one meeting, so long ago. At a stroke, the American automobile industry which had for so long been the cynosure of the world was cut off from the standards of the rest of the world. Maybe there were a few people, somewhere in the duller parts of small-town America, who were willing to adopt the AMA Party Line and "evaluate cars in terms of useful power and ability to afford safe, reliable and comfortable transportation, rather

than in terms of capacity for speed." But in the rest of the world, and including sports-car lovers in America, the result was simply to make American cars irrelevant. Speed on the track breeds safety and economy on the roads by encouraging nimbler handling, better braking, lighter weight and a more modest thirst, but the AMA edict effectively encouraged the nightmares of the late 1950s, overweight and ill-handling behemoths with braking systems a decade behind the times.

The immediate casualty of this edict was the Sebring Super Sport (better known as the Sebring SS), a derivative of the 1956 SR2. These special Corvettes were to the regular cars as Jaguar's C-type and D-type were to Jaguar's roadsters, and it is by no means impossible that the SS could have been developed to Le Mans standard. As it was, a defective suspension bushing – a simple assembly error – put the SS out of the '57 Sebring after only 23 laps, and further racing was effectively stilled by the AMA.

Nevertheless, unofficial factory support continued for Corvettes, and the second generation acquitted itself well at all kinds of races that included the Sebring '58 and the Pike's Peak Hill Climb. By now, though, there were plans afoot for a third generation of Corvettes.

In the Wilderness

The '58 Corvette looked as if it had been redesigned by a chrome fetishist. Ugly and unnecessary chrome "spears" were added to the trunk lid, and there were more unnecessary imitation louvers and air scoops all over the car: on the hood, either side of the grille, and inside the previously virginal "cove" or scoop on each side. Remarkably, the number of chrome "teeth" in the genuine air inlet at the front was dropped from 13 to nine. Twin headlights each side were neither a great advantage nor a great drawback, but a very significant disadvantage was 200 lb. or so (about 90 kg) of extra weight, partly a consequence of a body that was 9.2 inches (234 mm) longer and 2.3 inches (58 mm) wider. The only detectable styling improvement was the new tail-light treatment, which actually had less chrome and looked neater than the previous year's offering. As *Road and Track* quite fairly remarked in their contemporary report, the "improvements" for 1958 included "the corrosive influence of the 'stylists.'"

On the other hand, there were plenty of genuine improvements, too. Despite the ridiculous AMA ban on competition in any form, Arkus-Duntov and his chums realized that if they could sell the right Corvettes, ready to race "out of the box," then privateers and the media would do their advertising for them.

The hottest fuel-injected 283 cid engine, with the trick cam and high-compression heads, now offered 290 bhp at 6200 rpm, and a thousand cars were sold with this motor in 1958. This engine option added $484.20 to the $3631.00 base price, while "Positraction," the limited-slip differential option, was an incredibly modest $48.45 extra. The heavy-duty brakes-and-suspension package was a rather stiffer $425.05, and the four-speed transmission was an unreasonable $188.30 (what was unreasonable, of course, was that any sports car should still be offered in 1958 with a three-speed gearbox). "Ceremetallic" brake linings which offered somewhat more fade resistance than standard were $26.90. In other words, for under $5000 you could get a genuine sports/racer, straight from Chevrolet.

Everyone, racer or not, got the new instrument layout with the massive semicircular 160 mph (260 kph) speedometer and the other instruments in front of the driver where they could be seen, instead of being scattered all over the dash as they had been before. The drums were finned for cooling, and another option was vented backing plates with air scoops, motorcycle style. And if you then opened up the dummy holes in the front of the car, the brakes were significantly better cooled.

While there may have been some people who bought the Corvette because it now looked more like a 1950s American car, with chrome and various gewgaws applied, it is clear that the vast majority bought them because they were quick and fun. After all, this was the way that Jaguars and Triumphs were sold in England. The net result was that '58 was the first year that the Corvette program actually showed a profit.

In '59, the worst of the styling excesses were removed – the chrome "spears" at the back and the fake hood louvers – and sintered-metallic linings replaced the Ceremetallics. This meant smoother braking and no real need for brake warm-up – as cold Ceremetallics could pull mercilessly to one side or the other, quite unpredictably. Even with the extra weight, 0-60 times of 6.6 seconds were possible with the 290 bhp motor. Fuel consumption was, however, an alarming 14 mpg or so, close to 16 liters/100 km. That year, they sold 9670 cars.

For 1960, there was more of the same. Hitherto, even

the mighty 290 bhp fuel-injected motor had been handicapped with hydraulic valve operation. Switching to solid push-rods might have made for a tiny bit more noise, and undoubtedly entailed a little more maintenance, but in conjunction with an 11:1 compression ratio these top-end modifications liberated another 25 bhp, for a total of 315 bhp at 6200 rpm. Working downwards from there, you could have the same thing with hydraulic valve actuation at 275 bhp, a pushrod engine with twin four-barrel carbs and 270 bhp, the same with hydraulic valve actuation and 245 bhp, and finally the "cooking" version with a single four-barrel carburetor and only 230 bhp.

A light-alloy clutch housing for the manual transmission saved a useful 18 lb. (8 kg), and there was a long-range 24-gallon (87-liter) fuel tank option. Absurdly, though, the high-performance suspension package was canceled in deference to the AMA's earlier rulings. The everyday suspension was, however, upgraded, so unless you wanted to race your Corvette, you were actually better off. But there was still that feeble-minded isolationism, together with the idea that American cars shouldn't be allowed to compete with go-faster foreigners, even though the Corvette was a potential world-beater. It is difficult not to harbor the suspicion that other makers didn't want to compete, either with the rest of the world or with the Corvette, and that they were content with a prosperous home market.

The Corvette was not about to be homogenized, though, and in 1960, it showed that it was really world class. In the ultimate *Grand Prix de l'Endurance*, the Le Mans 24-hour race, one of the three Corvettes entered by Briggs Cunningham, and with Bob Grossman and John Fitch driving, finished eighth overall. In a competition with Europe's finest, including all kinds of semi-prototypes, a recognizable Corvette held its own. It may not have been a great placing, but for a privateer racing a car that didn't even have factory support, it was a magnificent achievement.

As a matter of considerable technical interest, this was done with an increasingly outdated design. The rear axle was still live, a distinct anachronism, albeit one that was shared with Ferrari. And the truly remarkable thing was that the engine was effectively all-iron, because even as recently as 1960 GM could not make a reliable, high-performance light-alloy cylinder head! Although alloy heads were briefly offered early in the 1960 model year, they warped when they got too hot. That, and quality control problems, led to

GM's dropping the option after only a very few had been sold. Light-alloy radiators did, however, make it for '61, with better cooling and half the weight of the old copper-core version.

In '62 came even more fun: an increase in bore and stroke to give 327 cid (5359 cc) and a base power output, with one monster four-barrel Carter, of 250 bhp. The fuel-injected top-of-the-line version now offered no less than 360 bhp at 6000 rpm. Believe it or not, Powerglide transmission was still available on the lower-performance engines, but it simply couldn't take the power from the larger ones. The body lost still more of its unnecessary chrome, too, and for many people, the '62 is one of the all-time greats. And then, in true Corvette fashion, just as they had ironed out the last of the faults, they decided that the whole car was getting a bit long in the tooth and it was time for a new model.

Sting Ray!

The name alone was enough to send a shudder down the spine, a shudder of anticipation, not unmixed with fear. The original Stingray (all one word) had been a racer, but the new Sting Ray combined totally radical styling with serious attention to going even faster.

To be perfectly honest, the styling was a little overdone in places. The split rear window, handsome though it might look in a show car, was sheer idiocy for a sports-racer. The dummy vents in the hood and rear pillars were unnecessary, and the value of concealed headlights has always been doubtful – small aerodynamic gains must be balanced against extra weight, complexity and likelihood of mechanical problems. And curiously, there was no means of access to the luggage space save via the passenger compartment, though the E-Type Jaguar and the Aston Martin DB-series seemed well enough able to accomplish such a modest goal. But what had happened under the skin was far more interesting.

The original McLean concept of setting the engine well back was followed, and indeed improved upon, and the front/rear distribution was a brilliant 51/49 per cent. The center of gravity was lowered two and a half inches (from 19 inches), and the passengers sat inside the ladder-type chassis rather than on top of it. Independent rear suspension kept the driven wheels on the ground, and reduced unsprung weight overall. Steering was a sluggish 19.6:1, and it was still recirculating-ball, but it was easy to change it to 17.1:1 by using secondary tie-rod mounting holes provided by the factory for precisely that purpose. Power steering was offered on the smaller-engine models and came with the quicker steering as standard.

There was much more metal under the fiberglass, but the 'glass itself was made thinner so the whole car was lighter than its predecessor. The new car was also four inches (102 mm) shorter in the wheelbase. Brakes (still cast-iron drums) were widened for a little more stopping power, so handling and stopping were significantly improved.

The motors were essentially the same, but the "no competition" rule was circumvented with the RPO Z06 handling package. Available only for fuel-injected models already equipped with the limited-slip differential, the $1818.45 RPO Z06 option brought you Al-Fin power brakes with sintered linings (Al-Fins had a finned alloy casing shrunk onto a cast-iron drum, for less weight and better cooling). The option also gave a heavy-duty front stabilizer bar, stiffer springs with upgraded shock absorbers, a dual master cylinder, and a 36.5-gallon long-range tank. Although this option was listed for both convertibles and coupés, it seems that it was only ever fitted to coupés. The 0-60 times with the hottest motor were now under six seconds, and top speed (depending on final drive ratios) was around 140 mph (225 kph). And at the Sting Ray's competition debut at Riverside on October 13th, 1962, it won!

In the '63 model year, 10,919 convertibles and 10,594 coupés were sold, so the '64s were only modestly altered: you don't change a winning game! The most important change was that the rear window was made one-piece, which was universally lauded by fast drivers but which made the split-window models into valuable collectors' items almost overnight. The fake air intakes disappeared, the ventilation slots on the pillars of the coupé were made functional, and the suspension was reworked with variable-rate springs and better shock absorbers. The interior was quietened (in response, it seems, principally to European criticism!), and the most powerful engines were given pretty much nominal power increases, with the maximum available now up to 375 bhp. Also, GM finally solved its problems with alloy wheels. The first options had been so porous that they would not keep the wind inside the tires, and so handsome light-alloy knock-ons were now available as an alternative to pressed-steel and distinctly tacky hub caps.

In '65, the Corvette finally gained four-wheel disk brakes. The drums were still available as a $64.50 credit delete option, but only 316 of the 23,562 '65s went out with drums – a mere 1.3 per cent. In the middle of the model year there was all the more reason why the disks were needed, as the 396 cid (6490 cc) "big-block" engine was added as an option. The "cooking" versions of this motor came with 325 bhp and 360 bhp, but in Corvette trim with 11:1 compression there was no less than 425 bhp on tap. Depending on the final drive ratio chosen, top speeds would be anything from the mid-130s (about 215-220 kph) to the mid-150s (250 kph). Heavy-duty clutch, suspension and radiator were needed to keep the plot cool and on the road, but despite the added weight of the monster new engine, the weight distribution remained at 51/49 per cent front/rear.

Then, for '66, GM pulled out all the stops and fitted the Corvette with the 427 cid (seven-liter) engine, apparently because Ford's 427 cid engine was doing rather well in Carroll Shelby's Cobras. The nominal bhp of the Corvette engine was the same as the 396 cid, at a mere 425 bhp, but there was plenty more torque and also a persistent suspicion that like some other 1960s manufacturers, GM deliberately understated the power so as not to upset the insurance companies – figures of 450 bhp were bandied about. Geared for acceleration, as most "muscle cars" were, the fastest Corvette could go from 0-60 mph in under five seconds (Road and Track got 4.8) and still hit 140 mph (225 kph). Geared for speed, it could easily exceed 160 mph (about 260 kph).

Admittedly, the Cobra was quicker both on the track and on the street. But there was a major difference. The Cobra was essentially a racing car that could (just) be driven on the public highway. It was harsh, noisy, stripped-out and one-dimensional. The Corvette, by contrast, was a grand tourer which could be raced, and which could even sometimes win, against the much less-civilized Cobra.

The last year of the Sting Rays was '67, and many saw the truth in the often said "the last shall be first." It stood first in Sting Ray styling, and almost all the pointless gewgaws had been removed. And with the unbelievable L88 engine and 560 bhp (on 103 octane fuel!) it was also first in performance. It was time to change everything once again.

The Sins of the Fathers

The fifth generation, introduced in 1968, was the longest lived of all Corvette designs to date, and yet in many ways it is the least distinguished. Although the styling was spectacular and widely admired, just about everything else could be criticized, and was. That criticism stained not just the '68s, but also a number of subsequent model years, hence "The Sins of the Fathers."

The wasp-waisted "Coke bottle" shape meant a cramped interior, and luggage space was also greatly reduced. The steeply-raked seat backs (33 degrees instead of the 25 degrees of the previous year) made necessary by the lowered roofline meant that driver and passenger alike constantly had to push themselves back up. There was precious little lateral support, either. A nonchalant elbow on the window-sill led to an elbow at ear level and even chiropractic bills. And quality control was very poor. *Car and Driver* actually refused to do a road test – they listed the problems with the car they had been sent, and declared that they were not interested in testing cars that bad.

Witless details abounded. In addition to those already mentioned, there was a vacuum-operated lid which covered the windshield wipers when they were not in use. Operation of this gadget was unpredictable almost to the point of being random. The nose used to lift at speed, but the stylists interdicted a proper air dam, so the problem had to be resolved using front-fender louvers and an undersized spoiler. The "Targa" style roof had to be sawn in half to create a "T-top," as the open version simply rattled and shook too much. The engine bay was narrow, and the grille wasn't big enough, so engine cooling was marginal. The response to that was to cut a couple of slots over the mini-spoiler on the front. With the small-block engines, this pretty much solved the problem except under very adverse conditions, but cooling on the big blocks was never fully sorted.

And the frightening thing is, all of these problems were clearly the result of giving the stylists too much say, and the engineers too little. It looked horribly as if the Corvette was about to be turned into a pretty-bodied land barge.

In all fairness, there were some engineering improvements. Drum brakes were forever consigned to the scrapheap, and higher spring rates reduced pitching. Wheels were widened an inch, to a meaty seven inches. The new suspension-and-wheels made for increased precision in handling, but also for a harsher ride, and if you ordered the power steering and the power brakes, you lost the precision but kept the harshness. The designers had also had to contend, for the first time, with federally-mandated safety standards that included items like non-lethal doorhandles and switches.

In short, it was still as quick as ever, but it had lost its way. It was not a real fire-breather like the Cobras which were then a recent memory, but equally, it wasn't a comfortable, grand-touring car either.

Fortunately for true sports-car fans, none of this seemed to upset the buyers. They paid for 28,566 cars, though it is hard not to suspect that the people who bought the new model were not quite the same as those who bought the previous model, and were probably more into appearance than function.

Continued sales meant, though, that those at Chevrolet who cared about function could concentrate on getting the car right. For a start, they spent $120,000 to get an extra half-inch of shoulder room on each side, and reduced the rim size of the steering wheel to allow more leg clearance. Apart from that, they mostly concentrated on quality control, on getting the car to work as it was originally supposed to, rather than like the version they had sent out to *Road and Track*.

They did not, however, neglect that fine old marketing concern of brute power. The small-block motor was stroked to give 350 cid (5.7 liters), while a 430 bhp big block was added to the lineup. An almost unbelievable range of final drive ratios was offered, too, from 4.56:1 (a drag-racer's special) to 2.75:1, which would have been ideal for long-distance touring at sustained speeds of 120-130 mph (around 200 kph).

Even so, the June 1969 edition of *Road and Track* discovered something potentially very unpleasant indeed for fans of "America's only sports car." They ran a four-way comparison test between a Mercedes-Benz 280SL automatic, a Jaguar E-type manual, a Porsche 911T and a 350 cid automatic Corvette, and not one of the four testers chose the Corvette as a personal favorite. All but one (who was a Mercedes admirer) chose the Porsche instead, which was $6418 instead of the Corvette's $6392 (prices as tested). In other words, the better car was only $26 more, and if you were a traditionalist who preferred a Jaguar, you would only have to find another $103 to buy the E-type. The Corvette's old "bang for the buck" reputation had all but ceased to exist, though admittedly if you wanted raw power you could still buy, for example, RPO ZL1, an all-alloy, dry-sump big block with 585 bhp plus other bonuses.

Why should GM worry? Corvette sales still continued to climb, at 38,762 cars for 1969. Fortunately, GM saw the writing on the wall, though, as there is a limit to how long you can sell any car on reputation alone. Something had to be done to re-earn that reputation.

They did it in all kinds of ways. The hotted-up LT1 variant of the 350 cid engine was advertised as having 330 bhp at 6000 rpm, but almost certainly had more, maybe even 350 bhp. And after a false start in 1969 it became genuinely available in 1970, while the 427 was enlarged to 454 cid (7,40 cc) and offered up to 465 bhp. The seats were reshaped to give more support, but weight crept up still more, to a very high 4000 lb. (1818 kg) or more.

From 1971, all kinds of interesting, though not necessarily encouraging, things began to happen. To begin with, power outputs started to be quoted as SAE net, which is comparable with (or even lower than) DIN, and takes account of power losses from engine accessories, mufflers, air cleaners and the like. And it was just as well that they changed their accounting base, because compression ratios were also lowered to allow all GM cars to run on 91-octane regular fuel, a nod to the emission control regulations that everyone knew were coming. The LT-1 dropped from 330-350 bhp gross to 275 bhp net, then again to 255 bhp net for '72. The five mph bumper requirement was cleverly met for '73 with a deformable, body-colored plastic section which would spring back to its original shape, a marked improvement on the Volvo-style battering rams that some people adopted. And then in 1973 came the so-called "gas crisis."

This piece of political nonsense was not really a crisis at all. What happened was simply that the petroleum producing countries of the Near East realized that they were effectively giving their products away, thereby earning less money than they could, and wasting their assets faster than they needed. But hysteria in much of the industrialized world led to severe speed limits – in the United States 55 mph became the federal norm – and then to a general loss of interest in high-performance motor cars. The overall effect of the "gas crisis" was entirely beneficial, in that it focused attention on efficiency.

If the Corvette had been coasting before, it all but went into hibernation now. The '74 Corvette was still a very powerful motor car, with a 0-60 time of 7.5 seconds and a top speed of about 125 mph (200 kph) in L82 trim. But the big blocks sputtered and died as an option, and it looked as if the Corvette was set to become a somewhat updated Morgan, a basically obsolete car with plenty of diehard fans (they sold 46,558 cars in the '76 model year), but only of marginal relevance to mainstream sports-car design.

And indeed, so it proved for some time. There were minor (and sometimes major) styling changes each year, and GM learned how to get more power from unleaded gas: the L48 of 1976 delivered 180 bhp, the L82 210 bhp. But the price broke the $10,000 barrier for the first time . . . .

Even so, the Corvette was safe. Sales figures tell their own story – 49,213 in '77, with the half-millionth Corvette coming off the line on March 15 of that year. Then a slight drop, to 47,887 in '78, but back up to 53,807 in '79. Another drop for '80, to 40,614 – though this was the year of the farcical 85 mph speedometer. Then 45,631 were sold in '81, a reasonable jump.

In the same year, 1981, Corvette production was moved to a new factory in Bowling Green, Kentucky. The brand-new, green-field, high-tech factory led people to suspect that the Sixth Generation might just be in sight, and so it proved to be.

Return to Glory

Although the previous generation of Corvette would drag on to 1983, the new '84 models were first shown in November 1982. And incredibly, they managed to remain true to the old Corvette tradition while still being serious, major-league, mainstream sports cars. And from the very start, the new Corvettes were incomparably better than the ones they replaced.

Styling was wonderfully restrained, and the stylists were not allowed to work their art at the expense of engineering. Just about everything was new, and there was a great deal which was either pure racing practice, or looked very like it.

To begin with, the old-fashioned chassis was replaced by the closest thing you could get to unitary construction in a glass-bodied car. It looked like a chassis with an integral roll-bar and spectacular firewall/windshield unit, though Chevrolet's description of it as an "integral perimeter-birdcage unitized structure" sounds more like something from the PR department than something from an engineer! One cannot help wondering if they ever actually saw the space-frame of the "Birdcage" Maserati.

The original engine was the 350 cid (5.7 liter) V-8, still anachronistically all cast iron and delivering a very modest 205 bhp (net, remember) at 4300 rpm, but a thorough weight reduction program got the overall weight of the car down to 3200 lb. (1455 kg) for a power-to-weight ratio of better than 140 bhp/tonne. The new body was vastly superior in aerodynamics to the old "Mako Shark" style, and the drag coefficient (C_d) of 0.34 was very respectable indeed, but together with the reduced frontal area it allowed very much taller gearing for high-speed cruising, while the improved power-to-weight ratio meant better acceleration than the older and ostensibly more powerful older cars. With the 4000+ lb. of the older design, about 250 bhp would have been required just to maintain the same power-to-weight ratio, and those are net bhp. The old SAE gross equivalent would probably have been close to 300 bhp. Extensive use of both cast and forged light alloys, including even a die-cast magnesium-alloy air cleaner, helped the weight-saving program.

To connect the power with the 16-inch wheels, there was a "4+3" gearbox, a four-speed manual with mechanical overdrive on the top three gears and some weird computer-control circuitry (which could be overridden) in both the overdrive and the gearbox itself. In order to squeeze through EPA gas-mileage requirements, under EPA test conditions the gearbox would simply take you from first to fourth. The whole setup was so complicated, and offered so few advantages, that many customers simply chose the four-speed automatic instead, until the new manual gearbox came along in 1988.

The brakes were big, ventilated disks on all wheels, which were all totally non-interchangeable. Like the tires, the wheels were unidirectional, which meant that left and right were not interchangeable, and they were of different sizes front and rear – 8.5 inches at the front, and 9.5 inches at the rear. They certainly put the power on the road, though! For normal use, the suspension was fine, and the Z51 package was a modestly-priced ($51) option for competition use, but too harsh for everyday driving. Steering was at last rack-and-pinion, at 15.5:1 in standard form or 13:1 with the Z51 package.

The car was also bigger inside, but smaller outside. It was 8.8 inches (224 mm) shorter overall, two inches (50 mm) shorter in the wheelbase, 1.1 inches (28 mm) lower, but with 6.5 inches (165 mm) extra shoulder room, slight but detectable gains in headroom and legroom, and eight cubic feet (about a quarter of a cubic meter) more luggage space. The seats were vastly superior to the previous version, even if you did not opt for the electrically adjustable "super-seats" with power lumbar adjustment. And on the coupé, the top was now a true "Targa," not a "T-roof" compromise.

On the original road tests, top speed was 140 mph (225 kph), 0-60 mph times were under seven seconds, and the whole plot was very sticky. *Car and Driver* reported a 0.9 g lateral acceleration on the skid pan, bettering the Ferrari, Porsche and the like. This was clearly a world-class car, but it was stuck with a certain amount of undesirable baggage. There was the long, boring previous generation, the apparently much less powerful engines, the weird 4+3 box, and the "Star Wars" digital instrument display. This last feature was all right in poor light, but could not compare with traditional swinging-needle displays in sunlight or in competition driving. It was the only real major error in the whole car, and enabled many people to dismiss the magnificent vehicle, then and there, as just another over-styled gimmick.

For 1985, fuel injection and a higher compression ratio gave a power increase of better than 10 per cent to 230 bhp, and the Z51 competition package allowed a genuine 150 mph (over 240 kph) to be seen on the clock.

For all that it was a vastly better car than the previous version, sales plummeted to a mere 39,729. The reason, though, was not hard to find. With a list price of well over $24,000, the Corvette was running into that most traditional of American problems, price resistance. The Corvette was too cheap to be exclusive, and too expensive to be readily affordable. Never mind that it was infinitely better value than many cars that were much more expensive, and that in many ways it was a better car, period. It just didn't sell as well as it should have done. Anyone who was smart enough (and, it must be said, rich enough) to buy a Corvette got one of the most incredible deals on four wheels.

In 1986, the price jumped even higher, to over $27,000. But that was the year that saw the introduction of ABS anti-lock braking from Bosch, probably the most important advance in braking since the invention of disk brakes, and comparable in importance with the first appearance of front-wheel brakes in the days when most cars had rear

wheel brakes only. It was nothing new as Jensen's FF had had it a decade and a half before in more primitive Dunlop Maxaret form, but it is still pure magic. Any vehicle with ABS stops faster than it has any right to do, under any conditions, and with full control. In the same year, alloy heads finally dragged the old V-8 into the 1960s, as well as saving 125 lb. (57 kg) and getting the weight just under 3000 lb. (1364 kg) for a power-to-weight ratio of better than 168 bhp/tonne.

The following year saw even more power – 240 bhp and 0-60 mph times in the 6.3 second range – but the coupé now started at $30,000 and the convertible was over $3000 more. The car competed on substantially equal terms exotica-wise, at twice the price, but sales fell again, to a mere 30,632.

The 10 bhp upgrade for 1987 was nothing remarkable, though the 17-inch wheels with their special tires reflected modern low-profile racing tire practice. The real fun started in 1990 with the ZR-1.

Go-faster engines were nothing new, the Callaway twin-turbo, with 345 bhp and 465 lb.-ft. of torque (compared with 330 lb.-ft. in stock trim) had been a more or less official conversion since about 1986, but in the meanwhile GM had bought Lotus. Instead of the sort of cynical badge-engineering exercise that many feared, they invited Lotus to "hop up" the 350 cid, and then agreed when Lotus told them that they would be better off with a completely new engine. As an aside, the '92 Corvette did have significantly more power (a fine even 300 bhp) from the older motor, but the new engine was something else . . . .

The ZR-1 was still a 350 cid V8 with a 90-degree included angle, which was nothing remarkable. But it featured all-alloy construction (including Nickasil bores), two overhead cams per bank of cylinders, twin 16-valve heads, and what amounted to a racing bottom end and racing exhaust, the whole thing fed by a computer-controlled electronic fuel injection system. A staggering 380 bhp was what they got out of the earlier versions, and 400 bhp was not reckoned to be out of sight, and yet this is a car which can be driven around town and can also be unleashed at anything up to 180 mph (290 kph) on the open road.

All of this went to rear wheels some 12 1/2-inches-wide (318mm) through a six-speed box (though maximum speed was reached in fifth) and sold for something around $60,000. A large amount of money, true, but a bargain next to most of its competitors. It was the flagship car of a flagship line, and the ultimate sixth-generation Corvette. It may even be the last traditional front engine/rear drive Corvette, which brings us to the Seventh Generation.

The Seventh Generation?

Since the 1960s, there have been rumors of a mid-engined production Corvette, and since the 1960s, they have turned out to be persistently wrong. At the time of writing, however, it would take a brave person to state flatly that the near future would not see the long-awaited totally new Corvette, and an equally brave one to say that it would supplant the ZR-1. After all, a 180 mph "classic" Corvette with a 0-60 time of maybe five seconds is a hard act to follow. Even the "basic" Corvette is a pretty remarkable car, the more so now that electronic traction control (essentially, a highly sophisticated limited-slip differential) has been incorporated.

It is also worth bearing in mind that the "old" Corvette was not a signal success in its sixth-generation guise, despite the general atmosphere of wretched excess of the decade which gave it birth. Sales were nothing like as impressive as they should have been, which might lead one to the unkind and depressing conclusion that it is easier to sell a relatively cheap car which looks fast than it is to sell a genuinely fast car which must, however, reflect its engineering pedigree in its price. Would it therefore be more reasonable to expect a policy of "the mixture as before," continuing the sixth generation with the ZR-1 as the flagship? Or a totally new prescription which has long been rumored to involve a twin-turbo V6?

The likeliest possibility, surely, is that the sixth generation will continue for a long while yet, perhaps with very much increased emphasis on overseas sales, while the "seventh generation" will at most be introduced alongside the more traditional automobile. After all, there was already a mid-engined sports-racing Corvette (which was at least nominally a two-seater) as early as 1964 – the CERV II. The XP-880 with its ohc Corvair-derived engine was another indicator of mid-engine possibilities, still in the mid-to-late 1960s, but far more significant because it could just about use the new ZR-1 engine, was the XP-882 of 1969. This wondrous beast used a V-8 engine mounted transversely and driving a Turbo-HydraMatic transmission by chain. The driveshaft ran back through the engine pan (sump) to the rear axle, and four-wheel drive would not have been difficult to arrange.

When he took the helm as general manager of GM, John Z. DeLorean knocked XP-882 on the head, on the grounds of cost, but then revived it again as a show car for the 1970 New York Auto Show, which led to its being hailed as the next Corvette, although of course it wasn't. Then came the twin-rotor Wankel version of the same concept, the XP-897GT, which was built on a modified Porsche 914 floor pan with a Pininfarina body. This played some small role in the emergence of the Chevy Monza 2+2, but was otherwise yet another non-starter. For the 1973 Paris Motor Show, an XP-882 chassis was re-engined with a four-rotor Wankel, which looked wonderful but died ostensibly because of reservations about the Wankel's thirst. And then came the Aerovette, which was essentially the long-suffering XP-882 with a conventional iron V-8 in the middle. Another stunning looker, and tipped as the sixth generation for release in 1980, it never got anywhere either.

Meanwhile, an aluminum-bodied XP-895 was yet another derivative of the XP-882, and this one was a runner, having been restored more or less as a private project by some Corvette enthusiasts inside General Motors, and actually taking part in the 1989-model press review at Riverside in 1988.

On top of all this, the Corvette Indy was a street-legal "concept" car based on the Indy racer, with a twin-turbo dohc V-8 of only 2.65 liters (161 cid), and Chevy showed that as early as 1986. Where did this leave the seventh-generation mid-engined Corvette?

The problem with any mid-engined car is that it is difficult and expensive to do well, and that it has limited appeal even if you succeed. It provides virtually no convenient luggage space, and therefore leans much more to racing than to road use. It is murderous to work on and to maintain properly, and if you use high-tech twin-turbo installations, you are just asking for trouble in more or less any automobile, the more so in one which is going to be subjected to the less-than-tender ministrations of the everyday mechanic. In fact, there is very little reason for using small engines and twin-turbos in the United States anyway, because you can get just as much power, and far more reliably, out of a bigger engine which is easier to maintain and where the slight loss of thermal efficiency is irrelevant in the light of incredibly low fuel prices. These prices are about one-third as high as in the rest of the affluent world, and, of course, there are no tax penalties for bigger engines as there are in most of Europe.

Lamborghini's Countach and Diablo showed the way for supercars with large mid-mounted engines, but not even their most fervent admirers would call them practical. The mid-engined Lotus cars are quick, but not the sort of brute quick that one associates with Corvettes, let alone Lamborghinis. The same is true of all but the most rabid mid-engined Ferraris. The mid-engined Porsches were simply failures, quite probably because their engines were too small and they were not quick enough. And besides, if the conventional Corvette begins in the high $30,000s and then just about doubles for the ZR-1, mid-mounting a big engine in some latter-day derivative of the XP-882 would probably double the price again. At the very least, it would have to be well over the $100,000 mark.

The logical thing to do, therefore, is to build a mid-engined Corvette with an even more powerful version of the Lotus-designed XR-1 engine – maybe 450 bhp – but to sell it alongside the "conventional" Corvette, which remains an infinitely more practical motorcar at anything up to about 150 mph and for any purpose other than out-and-out racing. By all means, let the mid-engined car be made in nominally street-legal form, because it could be sold at almost any price, but let it be in truth a racer which can be driven on the road. It is a strategy which seems to have worked for Jaguar, and there is no inherent reason why it should not work for GM too.

When the new Corvette roadster came out in 1953, it was so radical that many people wondered if it would ever see series production. It was almost what today would be called a "Concept Car," with its stunning GRP bodywork and its handsome wrap-around windshield. It abounded in practical touches as well as in style; the stone screens on the lights may look a touch vintage, but they are a useful feature on a fast road car. The straight-six engine was a bit too vintage, though; more power was needed.

By 1955, the Corvette was a real production vehicle (though still not being made in very large numbers) and it had a real engine – a V8, advertised as "CheVrolet" with a curious mixture of brashness and reticence. The vintage-style stone guards still remained, and the three-speed gearbox was equally out of date for such a forward-looking car.

In 1957 the engine reached maturity: the immortal "Fuelie" V8 with fuel-injection, and one bhp per cubic inch. The equally immortal "scoop" in the side of the body had appeared the previous year, when the lights had lost their stone shields. A 140 mph speedo graced the dash, and well over 130 mph was genuinely attainable with the fuel-injected motor, though maximum power took you right around the tachometer: 283 bhp was not developed until 6200 rpm. Many regard the '57 as the ultimate 'Vette.

It is hard to imagine today the impact that the '57 fuel-injected Corvettes had on the motoring world. Even the Europeans, who had been less than impressed with American cars since World War Two, had to sit up and take notice. No one could fault the Corvette's looks, a perfect blend of the brutish and the elegant, and now, no one could fault its power either. Fuel injection would remain essentially racing technology for two decades to come; the 283/283 could hit 60 mph in 6.6 seconds.

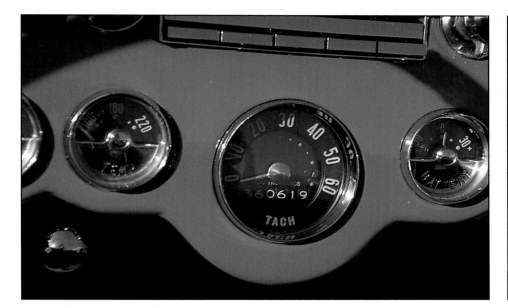

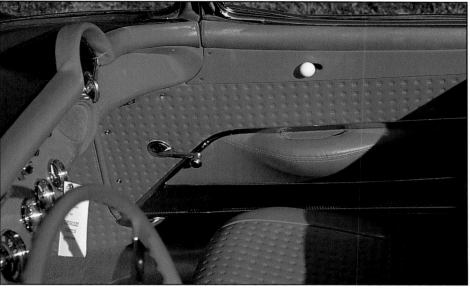

For 1958, purists bemoaned "the corrosive attentions of the 'stylists'," but by 1959 (when this car was built) some of the worst excesses had already been removed and the car merely looks exuberant today. Regardless of whether you thought the styling was better or worse, you had plenty of power. Even the base model 283 cid V8 delivered a useful 230 bhp, and the "fuelies" offered 250 bhp or 290 bhp.

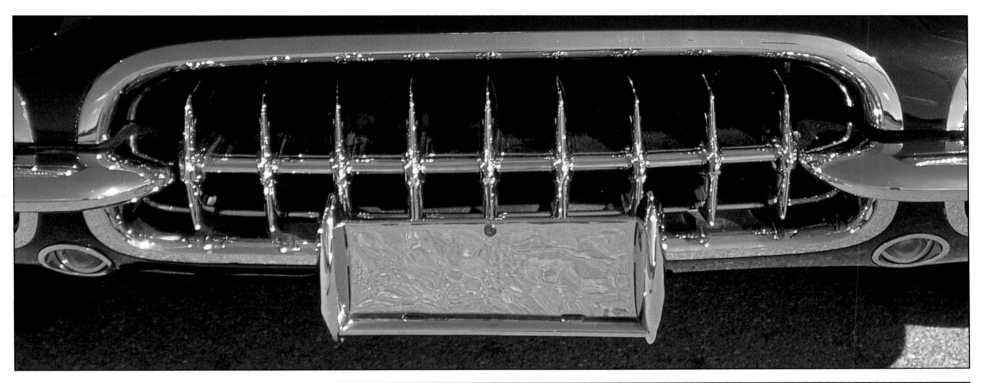

There were fewer chromium "fangs" in the "mouth" of the '58s than there had been in the earlier models, but the chrome-adorned "cooling slots" in the coves add nothing to the looks. The chrome spears on the trunk lid of the '58 were deleted for '59.

Like all Corvettes, the basic design change of 1959 was refined for several years. This 1961 roadster (also shown on the previous page) is a 275 bhp "fuelie"; the front-end treatment and the "twin-scoop" cockpit are very much like the previous years' models, but the rear treatment is very different. The crease running backwards from the top of the rear wheel arch, and the flatter, less rounded treatment of the trunk area, may look very dated today, but at the time it was very much the fashion. If you look closely at the speedo, you can see that a 160 mph speed has replaced the earlier 140 mph model; and the fastest Corvettes really did need the extra numbers on the clock....

For 1962, the last year before the Sting Ray, there were not many changes to the bodywork – though it has to be admitted that bright red suits the design very well, and makes it look fresh and exciting even today. The 327 cid, 300 bhp motor that powers this roadster was only one up from the base 250 bhp model; for those who wanted more, there were options of 340 and 360 bhp. Compare this with the 150 bhp "Blue Flame" straight-six of less than a decade previously!

There is no doubt that a hardtop provides better weather-proofing than a soft-top (always a consideration with Corvettes), and that it allows more trunk space. Visibility is vastly better, too. But most people would agree that a Corvette looks better, and is more fun, with the top down. If you were more concerned with practicality than poetry, though, would you buy a Corvette anyway?

The front end of the new '63 Sting Ray was rather a matter of "love it or hate it." It was very much more modern (in the idiom of the time) than the previous generation, though the whole treatment had been foreshadowed by the rear-end treatment of the earlier cars. What really set the new Corvette apart from everything else, though, was that incredible split rear window. As a piece of styling it was without parallel, but for rear visibility, it left a certain amount to be desired.

The new instrument layout was much neater and more modern than the earlier models, though the instruments themselves were somewhat over-styled; the huge chrome centers and bent needles on the speedo and rev counter are more Detroit than Le Mans. The choice of engines ran from a 250 bhp baseline, through the 300 bhp 327 cid carburetor-equipped motor in this car, to a 360 bhp "fuelie."

"You can't beat cubes," is the way Americans say it. W.O. Bentley was even more forthright: "If you want more power, build a bigger engine." The 396 cid (6.5 liter) motor in this 1965 Sting Ray delivered 425 bhp, and disk brakes were all but essential to retard its progress. The one-piece rear window replaced the split screen after only one model year, making the split-screen Corvettes great collectors' cars.

Inside the cockpit, the dials had become much more purposeful – a recurring theme with Corvettes, where the stylists seem to get their way with each new model, and the engineers and drivers then refine the car each year thereafter. The '65 Sting Ray probably looks most beautiful in profile (right), though from other angles it still retained a magnificent brutishness reminiscent of the earliest Corvettes (overleaf).

49

This 1967 Sting Ray is powered by the awesome 427 cid (7 liter) motor, which could propel the car to 60 mph in under 5 seconds. Some cars had "sidewinder" style exhausts, which were illegal in some jurisdictions and which in any case were unnecessary. What could improve on these looks?

Take away a hundred cubic inches from the 427, and you still have 327 cid and 300 bhp to propel this beautiful silver '67. It looks good from any angle but, like so many Corvettes, it looks, or at least

photographs, better in some colors than in others. Silver is particularly attractive, especially from the rear three-quarter view, but the view that most of us would choose is from the driver's seat.

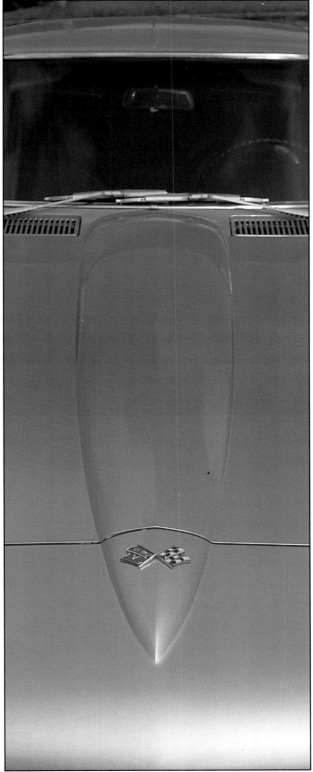

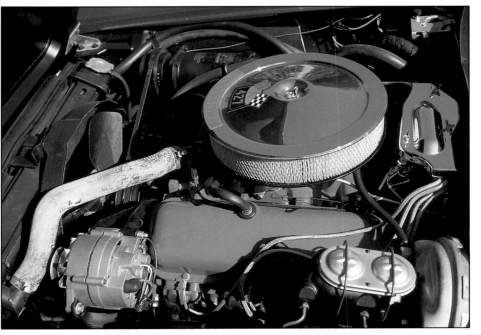

The Sting Ray coupé was such a *tour de force* that it somewhat eclipsed the convertible models, but they existed and, as can be seen from these pictures, they were very handsome. The lines are somewhat reminiscent of the Mercedes-Benz 190SL, but the American car has aged more gracefully; the 190SL was something of a parody of the 300SL, but the Sting Ray convertible was gloriously itself. This one is powered by the 427 cid engine; the interior already shows that happy blend of out-and-out sports and gran turismo which epitomizes Corvettes.

Once, many years ago, a Bentley raced the Blue Train; here the Blue Corvette faces no competition whatsoever…. The bloodline on the tachometer may only be at 6000, but the torque of the big 427 cid engine was in the locomotive class, and the solid chrome-ball four-on-the-floor transmits the power to the road most satisfyingly.

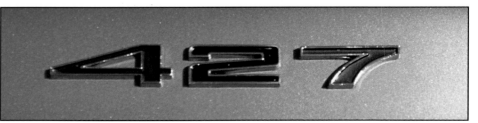

The Corvette as dragster. Taken together with the 427 cid engine and its 435 bhp output, the "sidewinder" exhausts have a certain inevitability. While this may not be the most sinuous or elegant of Corvettes, it has a sheer presence which cannot be denied, from the special wheels to the air intakes on the hood – and there are still thoughtful details like the spare wheel stowage (overleaf).

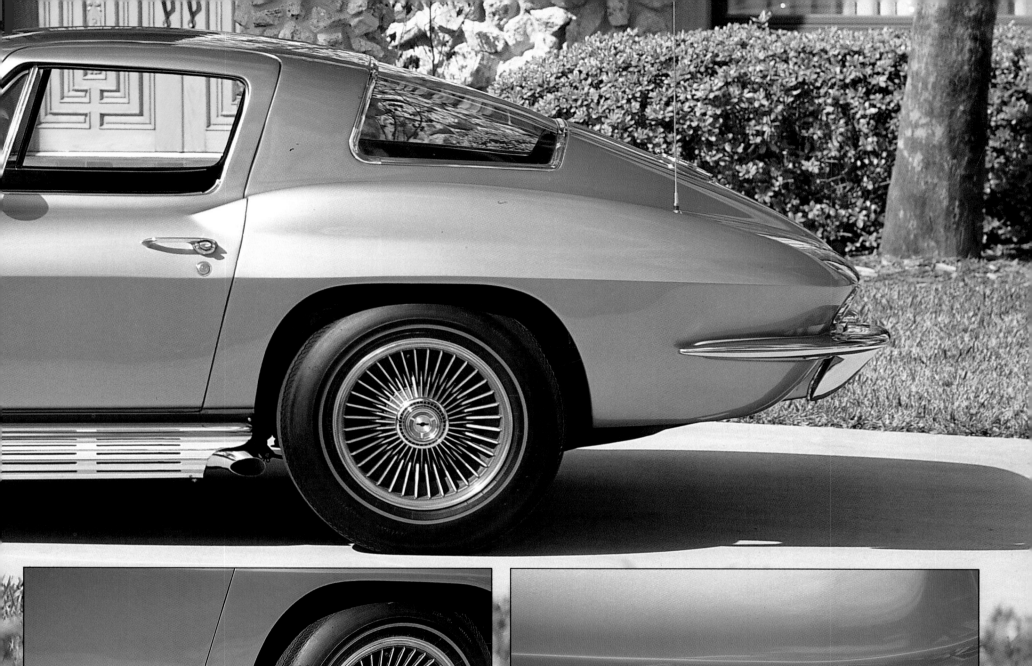
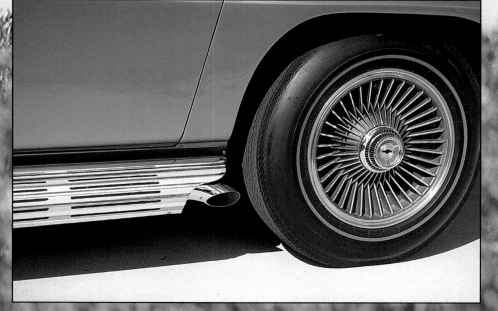

With the "cooking" 327 cid engine, and "only" 300 bhp, this 1967 Roadster (also overleaf) is still a very potent piece of machinery. The hood is arguably more elegant without the cooling scoops, and of course the 327 cid motor is significantly lighter than the 427, which allows better balance; but the relatively mild state of the engine is betrayed by the 5500 rpm bloodline, with a warning zone from only 5000 rpm. And look closely: those are not true light-alloy racing wheels. But even with these shortcomings, can you honestly say that you would not covet it?

Each new Corvette, like this 1968 coupé with the 427 cid engine and no less than 435 bhp, is greeted with howls of agony and rage by those who reckon that the previous series Corvettes were the best ever. As it is steadily improves, it wins more and more devotees until even the die-hards confess themselves to be won over to the new style; then, just when everyone agrees they have got it right, they change it!

There is, however, no doubt that the '68 Corvettes were not fully "sorted" when they were released to the public, and there were even basic design flaws. The handsome-looking interior did not seem to be designed to hold actual people; the aerodynamics and cooling were wrong, and there were details such as the concealed wipers which simply did not work properly.

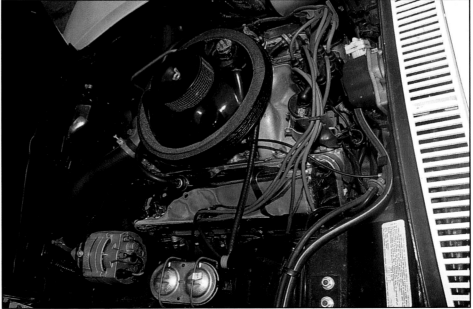

When in doubt, paint it red. It's a good motto for sports car manufacturers (it works for Ferrari!) and with any luck, the sheer style of the machine will disguise its shortcomings. The "T-top" on the '68 Corvettes was less fun than a real convertible or roadster, but it stopped the worst of the body shake, and a luggage rack has for many years been *de rigueur* on sports cars used for touring – except that the '68 Corvette was plenty big enough on the outside to be a grand tourer, and with luggage in place, rear visibility was zilch. The '68s were the cars that *Road and Track* refused to test.

By 1973, the build quality of the fifth-generation Corvettes had been improved out of all recognition. The cockpit was slightly less cramped, too, as a result of a very expensive redesign. Despite the gigantic 454 cid engine, though, the power of this blue coupé is a remarkably modest 275 bhp – partly because the motor was redesigned to run on unleaded gas, and partly as a result of power outputs being quoted as SAE net instead of SAE gross.

By 1978, when this Silver Anniversary model appeared, the fifth-generation Corvette had been in production for a decade and was getting long in the tooth. Restyling was only skin-deep, but given the so-called "gas crisis," many people were grateful that the Corvette survived at all.

The long drop snout looked – and was – purposeful, but it would have been more effective with proper aerodynamics to avoid nose-lift at high speed. There is a sort of vestigial front spoiler beneath the air scoops, but it is not enough. Likewise, the rear spoiler looks suspiciously like a cosmetic afterthought, and while the big rear window increased interior space and improved visibility in traffic, it meant that the interior overheated rapidly in hot weather.

"Indy pace car" can be a dubious honor, after all, it's strictly reflected glory, and the car does not have to go particularly fast or handle particularly well. It's a good excuse for a fancy paint job and some dramatic graphics, though, and Chevrolet is to be commended for keeping the Corvette in the public eye in 1978, during a long period of dormancy when it could so easily have been forgotten.

The 1982 Collector Edition was the last of the fifth-generation of Corvettes, and was very much a Grand Tourer rather than a sports car in the traditional fire-eating mold. The big 350 cid (5.7 liter) engine delivered a miserable 200 bhp, and the car weighed rather over 3400 lb., so the power-to-weight ratio was a mere 128 bhp/ tonne; still very respectable, but a long way from the rocket ships of yore. Interior appointments, however, were very luxurious indeed, and the "double nickel" 55 mph speed limit meant that power was adequate for American conditions – at least for those who wanted to keep their licenses.

Perhaps surprisingly, access to the modest luggage area was still only via the passenger compartment, and the big racing-style central filler was a reminder of the past rather than a statement of intent. "Cross-fire injection" may have sounded impressive, but the sad truth was that emission controls, unleaded gas, and an increasingly outdated engine design meant that the specific power output was a truly appalling 35 bhp/ liter.

The sixth-generation Corvette was first shown in 1982, but did not enter production until 1983 (the 1984 model year). To the uninitiated, it looked very similar to the older model, but it was an incomparably better car than its predecessor in almost every way: lighter, roomier, more comfortable, with a true "Targa" top instead of a T-top, and with vastly better access to the significantly larger luggage space. Improved aerodynamics meant that 140 mph was still in sight, even with the relatively modest 205 bhp motor; "Tuned Port Injection" was another of those marketing terms that did not actually translate into the power it promised.

Flipping up the big nose revealed a chassis, suspension and massive tires on unidirectional wheels, all of which looked well able to handle far more power than was offered at first, while the steeply-sloping windshield and Kamm-influenced tail hinted that with more power, the car could comfortably go a lot faster.

Although it was significantly more expensive than the coupé, the convertible (also overleaf) was a very handsome open fast tourer. When it appeared in 1986, it was chosen as the Indy pace car, and although this shade of yellow was the color of the Indy car, "replicas" could be ordered in other colors as well. In terms of sales that year, the coupé won hands down.

Pop-up lights are a necessary evil on many sports cars, in order to meet construction and use regulations governing the height above the ground of headlights. The car invariably looks better with them retracted, but on the Corvette there is the odd "inside-out" effect that they are "looking" at you when you open the hood.

With the new chassis, the Corvette could return to competition. Admittedly the "Corvette Challenge" was not a proper international racing series – it was based at the factory in Kentucky – but it showed that Chevrolet was concerned to get the handling and performance of the new car up to serious levels.

Corvette Challenge cars were not really very fast by the international standards of the time, with top speeds of just about 150 mph, but these were essentially road-going cars despite their internal bracing, roll-bars, racing harness and other paraphernalia.

Also, while 150 mph may be "not very fast," these Corvettes were not straight-line specials. They could actually be hurled around corners rather quickly – a far cry from the nominally faster products of some other manufacturers.

The 35th Anniversary Corvette was a much better car than the 25th anniversary Silver Jubilee model, especially at high speed; proper aerodynamics kept the nose on the ground, and 245 bhp propelled the car at up to 150 mph on a good day, with zero-to-sixty times well under six seconds. The all-white seats were inclined to get grubby rather quickly, though they provided excellent support for driver and passenger alike and were very comfortable.

Despite the murderous complexity imposed by the need to meet emission regulations, engine access was excellent. The specific power output of the handsome white-finished motor was still not very impressive, though, at about 43 bhp/liter. For its first half-decade or so, the sixth-generation Corvette remained more a Grand Tourer than a truly ferocious sports car. The ability of its chassis and suspension to handle far more power than was actually available meant, however, that it was a remarkably docile car to drive, and only a foolish or inexperienced driver was likely to take the car outside its "performance envelope."

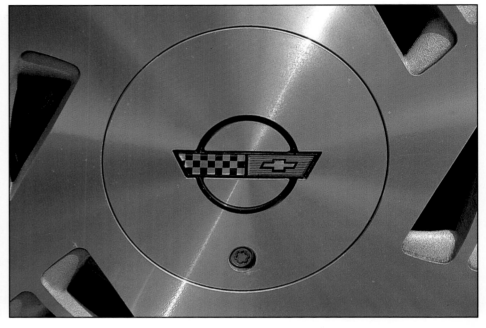

The stubby gear lever of this 1989 model controls no fewer than six speeds – a vast improvement on the overly-complex 4+3 gearbox of the early models, which was designed principally to finesse its way through EPA regulations. The power reaches the road through massive alloy wheels.

The Corvette authority Nicky Wright described the late 1980s models without the ZR-1 power plant as "a world-class sports car with an antique motor," and while this may be harsh, it is no exaggeration. The old Chevrolet V8 was never intended as an out-and-out performance motor, and although it gave a very creditable account of itself as the engine for a grand tourer, it looked very stale indeed next to its contemporaries. Though they might never require much more power themselves, the kind of people who bought Corvettes liked to know that a motor was available which allowed the Corvette to compete with Lamborghinis and Porsche Turbos.

At last, with the appearance of the LT-5 motor, the final piece of the jigsaw was slotted into place. Chevrolet were initially coy about the output of the Lotus-designed all-alloy V8, but it was generally accepted to be at least 100 bhp higher than for the previous version, with 380-400 bhp readily and reliably available if required in future. The six-speed gearbox now had plenty of power to transmit; the massive rear wheels could really get down to the task of laying serious power on the road, and anyone who was brave enough (and rich enough!) had a Corvette which could be steered with the accelerator pedal and the brakes, as well as in the conventional manner. Top speed was about 180 mph. Is this the ultimate road-going Corvette?

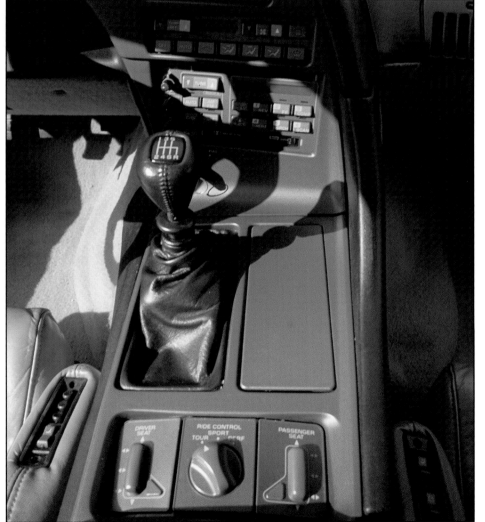